BIRD OF THE FARALLONS

Bird of the

Harriett Mandelay Luger

Farallons

Illustrated by Michael Hampshire

Young Scott Books

All Rights Reserved.
Text © 1971 by Harriett Mandelay Luger.
Illustrations © 1971 by Michael Hampshire.

Published by Young Scott Books, a Division of
The Addison-Wesley Publishing Co., Inc., Reading, Mass. 01867.

Library of Congress Catalog Card No. 72-155914.
Standard Book Number 201-09124-0.
Printed in U.S.A.

Dedication

"At this writing, only a few hundred of the thousands of birds treated for exposure to the oil are alive . . . 518 reported oil and chemical spills into San Francisco Bay have occurred between 1968 and 1970, according to the Regional Water Quality Control Board."

—*Audubon Conservation Topics—West*
February, 1971

This book is dedicated to those people who are doing what they can—cleaning oily birds, writing letters to Congressmen, appearing before city councils and in courts of law, and to those studying in schools and universities so that Ding's kind and all the other wild creatures in danger of extinction will not vanish from the earth without a trace.

ONE day the egg was too small, and he tapped gently at the shell. Then he slept until the pressure of his folded wings and cramped legs drove him to peck the dark wall again, with more force this time. He cracked the shell, but the effort so tired him that he fell back to sleep until the cool air seeping in and his swelling body awakened him, and he went to work with greater urgency. Pecking and sleeping and wriggling through the widening opening, it was two days before he tumbled out onto the rocky ledge into a world of guano and salt sea wind. The stink of centuries, overlaid with recent slime, did not bother him, but the wind cut through his sparse gray down still wet from the egg, and he screamed. He screamed because he was cold and starving and because he had never before seen the light of day.

Gently he was pushed and directed onto two black webbed feet, and he found himself in a sanctuary

between two black legs under a soft white warmth of feathers, sheltered from the cold, protected from the harsh light. Still he screamed his shrill, piping cry until another big black and white shape appeared before him, and he caught sight of a fishtail shining and dripping from a long, black beak. He seized the fish, which was as long as he, and with varied and prolonged contortions, managed to swallow it. Then he collapsed into sleep while his stomach rippled and gurgled as it transformed fish into bird.

Seventy-five feet below him the Pacific Ocean battered at the old stone cliffs men call the Farallon Islands, twenty-five miles beyond the Golden Gate. Every ledge was delineated by a line of erect, black-backed, white-breasted California murres, as close to each other as brooding space would permit. They had taken possession of all the crannies, all the burrows, the flat places, the niches, and the caves of the rocky

islands. Those not incubating eggs or sheltering babies pushed and shoved through the chattering, arguing crowd. There was a constant whirling and swooping of birds night and day in this late summer season as they came and went on family matters. When early morning shadows were shrinking and the shrill voices of the fledglings reached full crescendo, the greatest exodus to the sea occurred. Large numbers of small-winged, black and white murres dropped off the ledges and rocks at a steep angle in a long, downward curve. At the same time, others who had left earlier were returning, approaching their landing spots on a long, upward curve, flattening their bodies, spreading their feet and back-pedaling to check their speed so they would not dash themselves to death against the cliffs and rocks. Landing awkwardly on the narrow ledges, or in the rocky soil, they shook themselves, bowed to neighbors, and fed their young.

The salt wind almost always blew. The ocean sparkled and murmured, for the time of storms had not yet come. Sometimes the islands were enveloped in mist, and the fledglings nestled deep between their mother's or father's legs to withdraw from the raw damp, for their down, white below, black and white above, was scanty and stubby and offered little warmth. Overall the sun shone, the stars glittered, and the sky glowed and paled at day's break and day's end.

The chick did not watch, but he saw. He did not remember, but he knew. His down lengthened, and little feathers appeared all over him except on his wings. His parents began to leave him alone for short periods of time while together they foraged in the green water near the foot of the cliffs for his food. He squealed and quivered his naked little wings in loneliness and anger. Occasionally an adult neighbor leaned over and jabbed him with a razor-sharp bill, and his

fear and indignation knew no bounds. He almost split his throat screaming for his mother and father. When they returned with wonderful fish and shrimp, he forgot, as if it had never happened, everything which had occurred in their absence. Eating and sleeping and screaming, he quickly grew so large that his parents found it increasingly difficult to fit him in the small, warm sanctuary between their legs.

One mild, clear night about three weeks after he had broken out of the egg, he followed his parents, imitating their awkward shuffle through a crowd of palavering adults and anxious chicks. Suddenly, without warning, his mother and father spread their wings and disappeared. Then he heard their voices among a hundred others, distinct, but not close, calling to him in soft, coaxing tones, "O-r-r-r, A-r-r-r."

"I-r-r-rid? I-r-r-rid?" he replied anxiously, but they did not come back. He waited and he waited. Then, uttering loud objections, the chick shuffled toward the sound of his parents' voices. Suddenly he found himself on the brink of a great, black void which fell away from him as he stood on the very edge of the cliff.

"O-r-r-r, E-r-r-r," coaxed his mother and father, far down in the dark emptiness below.

"I-r-r-ridt!" he wailed, and fluttering about in panic, he lost his footing and slipped off into black space. Squawking and flapping his bare wings spasmodically, he rolled head over foot, down, down, down to land head first in the chill wet with a tiny splash, righting himself immediately. Shaking his head and sputtering, he did not miss one outraged scream. His mother calmly rose and fell on one side of him, and his father on the other. They murmured to him reassuringly, and his father ducked under the water and emerged with a piece of delicious seaweed which he dropped into the chick's wide-open mouth, and the chick forgot all

about the world of the cliff. He had found his second home—the ocean.

He went wherever his parents directed on the water. They continued to offer him food while his wing feathers grew. They escorted him to tidepools where they taught him to pick out from rocky crevices and their hiding places in the sand, little crabs and shrimp and sea snails. For salad there were beds of seaweed lying upon the water. He learned to take care of himself so well that he did not notice when his parents disappeared from his life.

Indian summer sparkled upon the ocean and in the sky. He was always among companions, mirror images of himself, flapping, diving, preening. When they came out of the water on the deserted beaches near the rocks, they looked like small penguins, hobbling, as they did, in an upright position. Their legs had joints an inch or so from their black webbed feet, making right angles

to the front, and they walked on those parts of their legs as well as their feet. Usually they kept their necks folded underneath their feathers on their breasts, and their heads rested upon their backs like pigeons, but when they were curious or agitated, they would shoot their necks up straight, supporting their black heads like periscopes. White collars, flowing out of their immaculate breasts, encircled their necks, thinning to narrow bands in back.

He had been trying out his wings for some time, flapping them and trying to rise off the water, but he had always fallen down on his belly. Then one day he flapped his small, stubby wings and rose so that only his feet touched the surface of the water. For several yards he "walked" upon the water, working his wings, and then he was in the air, and his second home, the ocean, sank away from him, as he skimmed over its surface, turning sharply from side to side, his bright

black eyes noting the sharp pricks of sunlight on the water, the changing blues and greens, the reddish shadow of a bed of algae, and dark, moving shapes beneath the surface of the sea. He found what he was searching for—the glint of a school of small fish—and he cut into the water like a spear.

He grew sleek and fat, hunting in the tidepools, skimming over the water which folded around the bases of the cliffs. He bobbed and flapped on the smooth, warm ocean and plunged his head into the water for whatever delicious morsel that chanced to catch his eye. He was never alone and rarely silent, usually mumbling placid *ow ow's* to anyone near him, or an occasional *arry* of mild protest. If he were thoroughly aroused he exploded into loud, bawling *KERAWKS!*

Imperceptibly, the sun delayed its rising in the morning, and the ocean cooled. On a certain day the

flock soared high into the air. It never occurred to him not to do likewise, nor did he spend time marveling that he had never flown so high before. He mounted the air, followed the bird in front of him, and took his place in the strong, straight line, one of several, streaking toward the south. His bright black eyes saw the stubby tail and trailing feet of the bird ahead, and he knew that behind him another black and white bird leaned upon the wind. He looked down on the multicolored movement that was the sea—the yellow greens of the shallows rippling into indigo depths; the piercing chips of sunlight dazzling upon the water. He caught the bright flashes of schools of fish, the dark thrust and turn of sharks and seals, and the roll and spout of the whales. His incurious eye saw sailboats scudding beneath him, scraps of white on the surface blue. He glanced at the freighters and tankers plying the coastal waters, their bows cutting the swells in identical thin furls of foam on either side, trailing gray smudges of smoke over immaculate wakes. One laid a heavy shroud over an expanse of ocean, crushing its movement, draining away its color, making it a cemetery.

Over his head the sun rolled across the sky; the wind combed through the cloudy blue; mist materialized from the water and disappeared. Secure as he had been between his mother's legs on the old ledge, he pushed the air behind him with a beelike whirring of wings. The murres would travel for a time and then, following the leader, drop down to the water and settle themselves to an interval of resting and eating. Part of the flock would remain preening and bobbing when the bird and his fellow travelers flapped their wings, walked on top of the water, and flew away. At each stop the flock lost members, and one day he did not glance up as some of his companions rose in the air to continue their journey still farther south.

The next eight months he spent floating on the swells and skimming over the surface of the water far enough out to sea so as not to be bothered by the shore's inhabitants. He dove like an arrow past the sunny green of surface waters past the dim twilight into the dark at forty fathoms down in pursuit of the particular shining little fish he desired. He flew equally well above or below the surface of the sea. Unfortunate was the fish he had marked for his meal. Rarely could it turn fast enough or dive deep enough to elude him. If by chance it did, there was always another to seize in his strong, pointed black beak, maneuver till he held it head first, and quickly swallow.

The nights overtook the days, and the air cooled. Rains pounded upon his head. The wind blew hard, and the ocean broke into pieces which jumped and crashed and splintered into spray. Serenely he rode the swells, sliding from heights to depths. When he was

hungry, he streaked into the dim, calm world below the surface and hunted. Several times a winter he would face into an Arctic wind, ruffle his feathers, and ride it out. His heartbeat did not quicken, his blood flowed calm. He was in his world.

Then the nights began to retreat, and the storms grew less frequent. Fresh damp fogs of spring settled upon the sea, and again the bird joined his colleagues to ride high above the water in straight lines. They flew and they rested. Fellow travelers joined them on their northward trip. One misty, cloudy morning he made a sharp descent and the customary upward curve to the rock where he had come out of the egg. He had not needed the murmuring and arguments of twenty thousand birds to guide him through the fog to the cliff. Back-pedaling with his feet and wings, he made the same abrupt, awkward landing on the ledge that he had watched his parents make the year before. He

found himself in a shoulder-to-shoulder crowd of irascible, garrulous birds, and he dropped off the ledge into the water among a less hostile, but no less excited, multitude. Great numbers of murres continually dropped into the water, while others rose into the air in flocks to perform strenuous maneuvers. Small groups spontaneously formed, running with great speed over the sea, flapping their wings, but never launching themselves into the air. The calm surface of the sea momentarily held the imprint of the figure eights, swirls, and curves they described in their intricate journeys. In a flash they dove, twisting and dodging, continuing their dance under water.

Infected by the general excitement, he rode the swells, gabbling, flapping his wings, stretching his neck. When a flock of murres rushed over his head with great urgency, he joined it, flying directly at the solid stone cliffs as if to go through them. At the last moment,

the flock curved upward, straight up, higher still, whirring their stubby wings, climbing into the sky until the islands were small and their inhabitants had melted into the rocks. Then, as if it were one creature, the flock wheeled and dove. The wind blew through feathers; bright shining eyes watched the approach of the great, calm, blue ocean, thousands of birds fluttering upon its breast. At the last critical second before impact, the flock leveled off briefly and immediately began another giddy climb above the islands, above the sinking sun, into the deepening sky. The activity on, above, and below the water continued until darkness disintegrated the flocks and the birds settled upon more prosaic pursuits.

The festivities continued for about eight weeks, gradually ceasing as spring revolved toward summer, when the mature birds nested on the cliffs and the yearlings spent the next two months on the waters

surrounding the islands, skimming, diving, socializing. The days shortened and again he mounted the air and took his place in the line of birds flying south, and he reached his own portion of the winter ocean.

He hunted and he played. He grew sleek and strong, and his belly was snow white, his back, wings, and head of blackest jet. When his stomach was comfortably full, he would float quietly, conversing with his neighbors and preening himself, shaking his head from time to time to excrete from glands near his eyes the salt he had drunk in the seawater. With his beak he would take some of his own waterproofing oil from the sebaceous glands near his tail (stretching his neck full length to do so) and burrow and pick among the short, thick white feathers of his chest. Then he would coat each long wing feather from base to tip, passing it through his bill. He would do the same for the tail feathers. If he chanced to catch sight of a delectable fish or a bit of seaweed, he would interrupt his grooming to dip underwater and indulge himself. Sometimes he stood on his head for a moment in his quest, his tail pointing to heaven, the rest of him submerged. Always there was good salt water under him, over him, around him—flavoring and lubricating whatever he ate; a cushion to rest upon, a table of plenty, a playground, a sanctuary.

He endured the darkness and the winds of winter without noticing them, and the rain left him dry and unaffected. When the dark receded and the days lengthened, he returned to the rocks where he had been born. This spring he refused to be displaced from the ledge where he had been born and instead added his voice to the furious babble and joined the fray. He pushed and bullied and jabbed, expertly dodging attacks and landing few blows. He found himself beside an attractive female, and with no preamble he

offered her his services. She refused him both verbally and by attempting to remove her person from his embrace. He was consumed by desire for her, and pursued her relentlessly. Neighboring birds stopped their wrangling to watch with interest the progress of the suit. He became more and more vigorous, and she ripped him with her beak. He turned away, for she had really hurt him. Immediately, she came around before him and squatted coquettishly. He jumped upon her, and the neighbors watched with craned necks and soft cries their lovemaking on the narrow ledge. For the second time in his life he tumbled off the cliff into space, but his passion not yet spent, he did not relinquish his hold on his bride. Together they plummeted almost to destruction on rocks barely showing out of the water seventy-five feet below. At the instant before doom, they separated and returned amicably to the ledge of their courtship.

They spent much time at first among the birds in the water at the bases of the cliffs, joining the exuberant water dances and joy flights. But the egg growing inside the mother bird dictated that they find a brooding place, and with much squabbling they laid claim to a small niche properly decorated with guano between two weathered boulders. In an absentminded way, they picked up nearby pebbles and dropped them in the niche and cemented them with their own guano, so that they would form a protective barrier for the egg.

The egg growing inside the mother bird weighted her down to such an extent that she could not fly. After days of patient waiting she deposited the egg (immense in relation to her size) on the hard rock where it lay cushioned only by the droppings of whatever birds had perched there through the ages. It was shaped somewhat like a child's top, one end being much larger than

the other, so that if it had been lying on the flat of the ledge and had been disturbed, it would have rolled in a circle. In color it was pale green with scrawls of lavender and purple. There was no other egg exactly like it among the thousands on the rocky island.

Now it was midsummer, but the mist lay upon the water most of the morning, sometimes barely lifting to clear the tops of the highest crags at midday. The ocean swelled and flattened gently, caressing the stone cliffs, and the tide spread like lace upon the shores of the islands. The bird would alight on the ledge, shake himself, pick at a feather or two, and hobble to the niche. He would bow and *ow-ow* to his neighbors. Since no one was ever silent, his greeting was returned as he made it. When his mate arose to take her turn on the water, their egg was visible for a second or two.

For thirty days either the bird or his mate carefully lowered soft white warm breast feathers over the egg.

They deserted it only at those times when the bold, voracious gulls, screeching their harsh threats, dove at the inhabitants of the cliffs. It did not matter that the gulls were hopelessly outnumbered, nor that if they were challenged, the gulls would retreat. Whenever they appeared, the black and white birds would desert their eggs, the males flying distractedly overhead, the females backing away, nodding their outstretched necks and bowing in distress and terror. The gulls would fly at the eggs, pushing them off ledges and rocks, gorging themselves on the destruction below. Often they brazenly pecked at the shells and feasted on the contents as they lay in the brooding places.

The egg of the bird and his mate was spared destruction, and one late summer day, their daughter broke her shell and emerged to the breezy, stinking world of the rocks. They warmed her and sheltered her between their legs, and they fed her. Sometimes she

would be deeply asleep when he scrabbled to a stop before the niche, a fishtail dripping from his beak. He would shuffle back and forth, waiting for her to awaken, exchanging glances with his mate, uttering a few muffled yodels—the best he could do with a full mouth. The chick continued to sleep, his mate continued to brood, and he continued to shuffle and gargle. Finally, with great reluctance his mate slowly arose and stirred her offspring gently with her beak. The chick awoke immediately, caught sight of the gleaming tail, seized the large fish from her father's mouth and laboriously swallowed it.

One warm, starry night when she had feathers enough to keep her warm and afloat, they coaxed her to the edge of the cliff, and she fell into the sea. They stayed with her until she could fend for herself, and then he and his mate dissolved their marriage. With the flock they skimmed over the water and dove after

the shining fish. They preened and gabbled companionably, rising and falling with the gentle swells, but the bonds which had united them against the others broke, and they merged back into the flock.

The days shortened and once again he mounted the air and took his place in the line of black, white-breasted birds flying south. Once again he hung between the sea and the sun, paying no heed to the sailboats, the tugs, the tankers pulling their wakes behind them or spreading shrouds upon the water. The porpoises gamboled and the seals slipped through the water; the fish flashed, and the seaweed floated over the sea. He arrived at his winter ocean on a hot autumn day when the wind blew from the land and the air was thick and cloying and lay murky on the water. When the discontented portion of his flock took to the air after their rest, he had buried his head below and hoisted his tail to the sky. He hunted and floated and preened through

the sunny days of Indian summer, under the dove-gray overcast of fall, and into the gales of winter. The sun lost authority, and the air grew cold.

It was during a time when the days broke late and ended early that a violent tempest raged and howled and blew all the hours of a long night. The bird and his companions sat imperturbably on the water, now at the bottom of a deep, wet valley, now on the crest of the swell. He caught the loud blows of the wind on his outside feathers, but he was warm and snug as he rode the chute down into another valley. Momentarily he disappeared in the boiling foam, but he bobbed up again like a black and white cork, always heading into the wind. A cold rain pelted his black head, and he ruffled his feathers for a little more warmth. Pushed in front of the gale, he and his colleagues suddenly slid into a strange calm where the great swells no longer splintered as they fell, and there was no foam, only surges of rising and falling motion. He turned to face into the shifting wind. As he moved, he felt the cold ocean at his breast and against his stomach. Tentatively he submerged his beak, immediately withdrawing it when he tasted the vile, heavy scum lying on the surface. He tried to swim away, but the strange stuff extended endlessly in every direction, so he resigned himself to sitting upon the water and waiting until this nuisance, like the storm, would pass. For the first time since he tumbled out of the egg into the sweeping wind of the Farallons, the bird felt cold, for the water insinuated itself into the warm, private places between each feather and touched his skin with icy caress. He became hungry and up-ended his tail to dive to his hunting grounds in the calm depth away from the storm and the sickening surface of the sea. But every fish he marked to satisfy his hunger eluded him. He could not dive quickly enough nor turn sharply

enough; he was heavy and slow. In a panic he returned to the surface.

The sky which had been a dark hollow of sound and fury lightened to a dull, lowering gray. At midday the rain still fell; the ocean still shattered into a million shifting gray fragments tipped with foam and spray. The sodden bird, blown by the wind, buffeted by the waves, sank little by little into the water, until even his wings were submerged. He could only wait, becoming more chilled and more helpless as the day turned to leaden twilight and disappeared into another long night of storm.

Finally with the breaking of another dawn, the gale blew the clouds away, leaving a clear, cold sky. The wind pushed great waves upon the beach, and the bird was carried into tidal waters. Unable to swim or to fly, he was borne by the strong high tide to the edge of the ocean. His wings beat ineffectually as the break-

ers tossed him up, hurled him down, and fell upon him, threw him on the wet sand and swept him back to sea. One breaker more powerful than the others flung him out of the water. He lay sprawled and dazed as the waves continued to jump at him. Leashed by the distant moon, the combers fell short, and gradually they receded into the Pacific Ocean. Though the wind blew brisk and sharp, the sun climbed higher and warmed the cold, blue Southern California sky. He folded his wings, tucked his webbed feet under him, and regarded the watery world which had rejected him. His eyes, his nostrils in his long, black beak, the very marrow of his bones told him that food abounded just beyond his reach—the darting fish, the delicate shrimp, the succulent seaweed. He was very hungry. He sat shivering with his feet under him and his wings folded, and he watched the blue-green sea smashing into foam, and he waited.

T HE storm, which two days ago had rolled in from the sea, blowing the air clean of smog, now thundered in great clouds to the east on its way across the continent. The sky was bright and cold, and the sun, nearing the western horizon, laid a sparkling roadway on the water. The collie ran from shore to surf and back in wide arcs, challenging the breakers, snapping at them, herding them back to the ocean where they belonged. He spied the bird and stopped stock still, ears erect, one forepaw raised uncertainly. Looking over his shoulder at the youth striding along behind him, he exploded into brave barking and made feinting charges at the bird. His master squatted by the oily, disheveled creature.

"Man, you're just about totaled," he said. Carefully he picked up the weakly struggling bird. "Don't panic, dingdong. I'm an old pigeon man."

He cut across the sand away from the water, climbing the dune to the street where a mahogany brown Jeep station wagon with truck directionals on the square front fenders and orange flowered curtains at the windows was parked at the curb. It was his first car. He had just bought it with his own money, and his father had made him a present of the paint job for his seventeenth birthday. He examined it sharply with his eyes as he unlocked the door. Lucky insinuated himself in the space behind the back seat, avoiding the upholstery. The youth dumped a pair of new tennis shoes from their box on the front seat and gently placed the bird in it. He started the car, his face reflecting concentration, then satisfaction, as he pulled smoothly into traffic, trailing a small, temporary cloud of transparent, blue exhaust.

He came into the kitchen, the box in his hands. His father was standing by the back door watching his wife and daughter as they fixed dinner. "What have you got there, Allen?" he asked.

"An oil-soaked bird. There must be a slick around. The sand is black." Mother and daughter left their preparations, and all four people looked at the shoe

box. The dark, bedraggled head shot up and swivelled like a periscope, inspecting every corner of the kitchen with a bright gaze. Allen lifted the bird out of the box. Two webbed feet gently beat the air.

"Hey, you dingdong, hold still!"

"Who are you, bird?" asked Eleanor, Allen's younger sister. "Where is your home?" The bird regarded each of them in turn. Mrs. Charles timidly reached out to touch a black webbed foot.

"You're ice cold!" she said. "Allen, how are we going to get him warm?"

Allen went to the garage and got a carton box which he brought back to the kitchen and put on the washing machine. He placed a mechanic's light—a bulb in a little wire cage—on the bottom and set the bird as close to it as possible.

"I'm going to phone Clyde Larson," Mr. Charles said. Clyde Larson was a friend, a biologist, who taught in a nearby college. He came right over.

"What you've got here, Allen, is a California murre,"

he said, "the most common offshore bird along the Pacific coast from Alaska to Baja California. Right now he's got two big problems—food and oil. Let's get the oil off him first."

The kitchen took on a hospital air, Mr. Larson and Allen becoming a team of doctors uniformed in aprons. Mr. Larson gently but thoroughly washed the bird with castile soap while Allen held the sodden handful of feathers dominated by a bright button eye. Then he blotted the bird as dry as he could with a white bathtowel, dyeing it with dirty splotches. When Allen set the bird down by the mechanic's light, he fluffed his feathers till they stood on end, and he looked like a big, black pine cone. Mrs. Charles offered him canned sardines, but he refused them, shaking his head decisively. He nestled close to the light, and his eyelids drooped. He looked comfortable. Mr. Larson instructed Allen to get some fresh anchovies from the bait store on the pier as soon as possible, and he went home.

The next day was Saturday. Though Allen had been

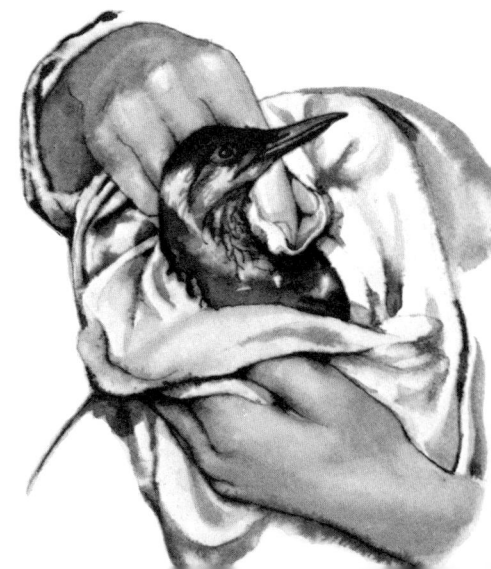

on a late date the night before, he came into the kitchen while early morning dusk still lay heavy on the stove and draped the cupboards with gray, and the window was a square of bright twilight. He tiptoed toward the warm, golden glow of light drifting above the carton. The bird had been asleep, his head turned on his back, beak buried under his feathers, but he stood up when Allen appeared. He tried to spread his wings, but the box was too small, so he refolded them and regarded Allen brightly. Allen picked him up and held him at eye level. They stared at one another.

"Ding, baby, you're a champ," the boy said.

"Is that what you're going to call him?" Eleanor had come up behind him. "Want some breakfast, Ding?"

"Let's go get the fish," said Allen returning the bird to the box. Eleanor ran her hand lightly over his head and down his back. "Ding, you're beautiful."

They got their jackets and ran out into the chilly morning. The sun had just freed itself from the eastern horizon, and shadows lay long and thick on the lawns and between the houses. It was very quiet. They ran to the Jeep parked in the driveway. Allen extracted a torn T shirt from under a seat and wiped the car with the care of a handler grooming a racehorse. Then they drove away through the cool, damp morning, emitting fat puffs of steam from the exhaust.

When they returned to the house, Eleanor was kneeling on the back seat of the Jeep facing the rear, clutching the side of a huge TV carton which filled the back of the car and extended beyond the lowered tailgate. She and Allen wrestled it through the front door, thumping and scraping up the stairs, through the hall, and into Allen's room where it covered half his floor. He would have to squeeze to get to his clothes closet and would not be able to reach his record player at all. They brought Ding and his light upstairs and installed them both in the big carton. Mr. Charles stamped into the room.

"What's going on in here?" he shouted. "Can't a person sleep on a Saturday morning?"

"Here, Dad, you give him the first fish." Eleanor quickly offered her father the plastic bag filled with slippery, silver anchovies.

Ding stood under his light which had been hung overhead, stretching his wings and examining the blank, brown walls of the new carton. Mr. Charles leaned over the side and dangled an anchovy above his beak. He snatched it voraciously, and shaking his head, deftly maneuvered it in his bill, swallowing it headfirst. The three people bending over the side of the box cheered, and Mr. Charles offered another fish. Ding eyed it, but made no move to seize it. He shook his head in vigorous negatives and made chewing motions with his beak. He turned away and lowered his chest to the floor.

Mrs. Charles ushered Clyde Larson into the room. They had not heard the doorbell nor his ascent up the stairs.

"How is he?" he asked. "I brought him some anchovies."

"The supply isn't the problem," Mr. Charles replied. "The dumb bird won't eat."

Mr. Larson took the bird out of the big box and examined him carefully. Then he handed him to Allen. "He probably can't eat too well out of water," he said.

While Allen held Ding, Mr. Larson forced open the long, black bill and inserted an anchovy, headfirst, as far down Ding's throat as possible. It vanished. Allen had poured seawater into one of Lucky's green plastic feeding bowls, had floated seaweed on it, and set it in a corner of the carton on a rubber shower mat. When Ding had swallowed the second fish, Allen put him down by the green bowl. He ignored it. Allen pushed his head down, submerging his beak in the water. He drank deeply, blowing bubbles through his nostrils, poking and probing in the seaweed, tossing it around and splashing the floor by the bowl.

"I don't think he knew that was seawater," Allen said in surprise. "Hey, stupid, that's what you live on!"

"He's used to the whole Pacific Ocean," said Mr.

Larson. "He doesn't know what to do with only a bowl of it."

He slid six anchovies down the pale, pink opening, and six times Allen dunked Ding's beak into the water. They concluded he had had enough when a bit of the tail of the sixth stuck out of the corner of his bill.

From then on the bird gave Allen plenty of opportunity to drive the mahogany-colored Jeep. He had to go to the bait store on the pier several times a week; sometimes he made additional trips to the shore for seawater. He drove to every library in the area to consult the references Mr. Larson had given him. He became an authority on California murres and usually expounded on them at dinnertime.

"Their biggest rookery—a rookery is a breeding ground," he explained pompously, "is on the Farallon Islands just outside the Golden Gate. The Forty-niners liked the taste of murre eggs so much they almost exterminated the birds. Those guys were all over the islands gathering eggs, hundreds of thousands at a

time, and they sold them for a penny apiece. The government had to stop them."

Allen and Eleanor would bring friends to the perpetual winter twilight of Allen's room to see the black bird with the dingy brown breast. He would be dozing listlessly, his head upon his chest, but would snap to attention when guests appeared, getting to his feet, stretching his wings, then folding them neatly. They fed him as often as they could get a fish down his throat. One day he consumed sixteen, about half of them by himself, shaking his head negatively after each one, then eating another.

He preened himself thoroughly. He would twist his head, rubbing it on his back and wings to coat them with his own waterproofing oil. His feathers began to shine. Mr. Larson was delighted with their improvement. He had learned that vegetable oil was effective in cutting the petroleum, and almost every night Allen sat on the floor in the kitchen and dipped a toothbrush into a little bowl of salad oil and brushed it on Ding's feathers. Sometimes Eleanor held the bird, but often she had homework or had to wash her hair, and then Mr. Charles sat on the floor holding Ding.

"He's beginning to look like a penguin," he observed.

"Murres are auks, the northern counterparts of penguins," Allen told him. "Auks are smaller, and they are strong flyers. Penguins can't fly." Allen took the bird from his father and wiped the excess vegetable oil onto the stained bathtowel.

"Look at that!" he said, holding up the blackening towel. "Those oil guys should have to clean up all the oil-soaked birds with their tongues!"

"You're a pretty good customer for the gasoline that comes from that oil," his father observed.

The bird's body fattened, and his feet were always warm. As he grew stronger he was harder to feed. Eleanor's wrists were scratched from his claws, and Ding had taken to whipping his head around so violently that Allen was unable to open his beak. They had to enlist the aid of Mrs. Charles.

"I'm busy," she grumbled, but she carefully collared her hand around Ding's neck just under his head. He worked himself into a frenzy of protest.

"KERAWK!" he honked in indignation.

"I wonder why he is so hard to feed," Allen mused that evening as the family sat before the fire in the living room.

"How does he eat in his own world?" Mrs. Charles asked.

"He hunts for his food. He chases it." Allen said.

Mr. Charles looked at his wife. "What an intelligent question, Helen! Sunday we'll get him live fish. He can catch them in his bowl!"

A disturbing wind coming off the choppy gray ocean swept through the city, rattling windows and bending trees, emissary of an approaching storm. Clouds moved in and joined to mark the area of its domination. Then the rain came, sometimes wind-driven, sometimes falling straight from the sky. Old cars became new again, their colors freshened by the rain. The Jeep glowed like a dark jewel, blinking its amber directionals and trailing momentary plumes of pearly exhaust. Ding, surrounded by the dun-colored walls of his TV carton, its dry, level floor under his breast, drowsed under his light while the rain drummed on the roof, gurgled down the rainspouts, and dripped off the eaves.

On that gray, wet day, Mrs. Charles came in to vacuum Allen's room, but confronted by the smelly welter of buckets, five-gallon containers of seawater, and the gigantic carton, she gave up.

"It stinks of fish in here," she said to Ding, "and everything is a horrible mess because of you." When she addressed him, Ding stood up, watching her with his bright, black eyes. She leaned over the side of the box and ran her forefinger over Ding's smooth, warm head and down the sides of his neck. He leaned on her finger as she alternated it from side to side. When she stroked under his beak, he held his head high and half closed his eyes. Mrs. Charles lingered, bent over the carton box, forgetting her housecleaning.

That afternoon, however, she gave Allen an ultimatum. He tried to enlist his sister's aid in helping him clean his room.

"Are you crazy?" Eleanor asked incredulously. Then she reconsidered. "O.K. I'll take care of Ding."

She carried him downstairs. He came to life, alert and inquisitive in the space and color of the kitchen. His webbed feet and "elbows" clicked across the linoleum. His periscope head twisted and turned and bobbed, and he peered into every corner, behind the stove, the washing machine, and under the sink. Then he pattered rapidly toward the dining room. Eleanor barred his way and turned him around but he would not be deflected. She carried him to the opposite end of the kitchen, and again he hurried toward the dining room. A battle of wills developed, and Eleanor won out only because she took him in her arms and carried him upstairs. She asked Allen, moving a dustcloth around the various objects on his desk, "Do you think he knew he was running toward the ocean?"

Every day thereafter Ding had an outing. As soon as the rain stopped he was taken into the back yard, causing Lucky, broadcasting his heartbreak to the world, to be imprisoned in the garage. At first Ding stood by the back steps where they set him down, stretching his wings and reconnoitering in every direction. Then he explored beneath the dripping shrubs, poking his long beak among the leaves and into the damp earth. He tried a blade of wet grass for taste and rejected it. Suddenly he flapped his wings and ran the whole length of the yard high on his toes.

"They launch themselves into the air from cliffs," Allen said, and he tossed the bird from shoulder height. Although Ding beat his wings vigorously, he fell like a lead weight, landing on his chest. He struggled to his feet and continued to run on tiptoe, beating his wings. The wind blowing off the ocean brought urgent messages to him.

"Not yet," Allen told him, and carried him back into the house.

The following Sunday was a day misplaced from the other side of the year. The sun showed summer strength and splendor, and the breezes, mild and soft, ambled and hesitated. According to plan, Allen drove his parents to the pier to get some live food for Ding to chase in his bowl. While they were gone, Eleanor carried Ding to the front yard, for she knew that people would be out to bask in the sunshine and that Ding would draw them like a magnet. Gradually a crowd gathered on the Charleses' lawn to watch Ding waddle on his "elbows" and his persistent half-running, half-flying attempts to get to the Pacific Ocean a couple of miles to the west. A group of children, returned from a morning of surf-fishing, offered him little pieces of bait shrimp which he graciously accepted. He was very active and entertaining, preening and flapping and bobbing his periscope head. At the height of the merriment a big black Labrador retriever materialized and confronted Ding eyeball to eyeball. Ding remained calm, but the crowd galvanized into action, waving its

forty arms and making a terrible noise, and the frantic animal fled, tail between its legs.

   Meanwhile, at the pier, Mr. Charles bought a dollar's worth of frisky, silver anchovies in a bucket which Allen placed in the rear of the Jeep while they went down to the shore to get seaweed and to fill a five-gallon jug with fresh seawater. Lucky harried the breakers unmercifully, and they found seaweed with fat, brown, leathery leaves and thick tubular stems and another kind that looked like coral lace. They also gathered a few little crabs and some sea snails for Ding's pleasure. They sweated under their winter jackets as they struggled up the dune to the street. When Allen opened the door of the Jeep, it was as if he had opened the door of an oven. Most of the anchovies floated motionless. A few wriggled languidly. Mr. Charles got excited.

   "They're dying! They need oxygen!" he shouted. "We'll have to oxygenate the water with the tire pump! Let's GO!"

"You can use the vacuum cleaner as a blower, you know," Mrs. Charles suggested as the Jeep scuttled for home. "Turn the canister upside down and attach the hose. Now, Allen, don't go so fast."

They squealed to a stop in front of their house where the neighborly crowd admired Ding resting on his stomach on the grass. They looked up as the car doors burst open.

"What's up?" asked one man.

"Have to oxygenate the fish!" Mr. Charles shouted on the run toward the house. Impressed, the crowd deserted Ding.

"Carrie's on the phone, Mother. It's important." Eleanor, coming out the front door, bumped into Mr. Charles, who was trying to get in. He brushed past her, returning to the front porch with the vacuum cleaner.

"She said to turn it upside down, didn't she?" Mr. Charles bellowed to Allen. The neighbors, waiting to see the fish oxygenated, watched half the anchovies and water vanish into the vacuum hose.

Meanwhile, Ding, high on his toes, vigorously flapping his wings, was three houses down the block on his way to the Pacific Ocean.

The days passed, and Ding was well into his second week in the high-walled carton in Allen's room. He was far from immaculate, but his chest and belly were recognizably white, and he was strong and alert. Once he ran from one corner of his box diagonally across to where Allen dangled a fish and snatched it from his hand. He loved to drink water as it fell while being poured from the big container into his bowl. He would thrust his beak into the stream, shaking and splashing, working his beak with lightning-fast chewing motions. Long after he had taken any water he would shake his head and speckle the sides of his box with white spots of salt excreted from glands near his eyes.

One day while Ding was sitting grumpily in the kitchen, Eleanor surrounded him with a three-way mirror. For ten minutes he bowed silently to first one then another of the birds. He seemed to be seeking

something. Finally, he lost interest and settled down on his stomach, yawning in boredom.

That evening Allen was in his room doing homework. It was very quiet. Allen had not bothered to draw his blind, and a bright, cold moon thrust its light through the window and into Ding's box. A loud scrambling caused Allen to jump up. He found Ding running from corner to corner, flapping his wings.

"Are you trying to tell me something?" Allen asked the bird standing in the middle of his box, looking at the boy intently. He reached for Ding and carried him downstairs, stroking his back.

"I think Ding's ready," he told his parents. Mr. Charles phoned Clyde Larson, who said he would be over the following night to give Ding a bathtub test to see if his feathers were sufficiently waterproofed for return to the ocean.

The next night in the antiseptic glare of the bathroom, Ding's beating wings seemed to fill the tub. He attacked the porcelain frantically, searching for a way

out. When he tired, he sat upon the water, wings partially spread, watching the people who watched him. Then he splashed and scrambled and beat his wings again. And again he floated on the water. Finally, Mr. Larson picked him up, carefully examining his wings, probing among the thick, light feathers on his breast and the glossy dark ones on his back.

"I think you can make it, old boy," he said. He turned to Allen. "Even though he can't fly yet, he will probably get his strength back more quickly in his own world." He blotted the bird with the towel, by now almost completely black. Ding had left a thick, greasy ring around the tub.

"I thought I got most of the oil off," Allen said.

"He was soaked in it," Mr. Larson replied.

When Ding was placed in his box, he preened industriously. He fluffed himself so thoroughly that the pink skin showed between his feathers, now glossier than they had ever been.

"I hope he can find his buddies," Allen said, thinking

how lonely the ocean, how cold the wind, and how dark the night for one bird alone.

"I'm not going," Mrs. Charles said. "I don't want to see him put into the water."

Saturday morning early the Jeep carried Mr. Charles, Mr. Larson, Allen, and Ding in a small carton, back to the beach. As they approached the ocean, Ding became restless, beating his wings against the sides of the box.

It was between storms, a clear, sunny, briskly windy morning. The beach was a great emptiness of sand and sky and an endless line of crashing combers—and one small, black bird. He was unable to fly, and tumbled along on his ridiculous legs, wings outspread, toward the water. Allen picked him up and placed him where the tide would carry him back to sea. The undertow sucked him into the foaming surf, and he vanished, then reappeared, vanished and reappeared again, a black scrap tossed and stomped by the breakers. For the second time in his life he was cast out of his world onto

the shore. Allen ran to rescue him, picking him up tenderly and wrapping him in the black towel. The bright eyes were half open, the feet icy cold. They brought him home to his TV carton and set him close to his light.

Ding remained listless. The stove and the washing machine no longer interested him; he did not respond to the soft gray winter sky or the fresh, damp wind. No longer did he run toward the west. He sat on the grass or the kitchen floor or in his box, his chest down, his head between his shoulders. After a few days anchovies would no longer slide down Ding's throat; or once down they would not stay. Allen checked him often, even awakening from sleep to stand by the side of the TV carton.

"At least you're no worse," Allen said to him once in the middle of the night. Then, as the shade flapped loudly against the window and the bird's head shot up, he added reassuringly, "Don't get scared, Ding, baby, it's just the wind. There's a storm coming."

The ocean was breaking up. The whitecaps slid into troughs and climbed swells. Seabirds ruffled their feathers and faced into the wind. A sprinkle not strong enough to dimple the surface of the water hung in the air; then from the low, water-heavy clouds covering the sea and the coastland, the rain began to fall. It pelted the heads of the floating birds; it packed the sands of the deserted beaches; it painted bright reflections on city streets; it drummed on the roofs of houses.

The next morning, Saturday, Ding's feathers were dull; he trembled constantly and breathed heavily. Allen drove the Jeep through the rain to the pet store for antibiotics and to the bait shop for shrimp, both of which he forced down Ding's throat.

"Let him be," Mrs. Charles said as she held the trembling bird who tried to escape the medicine dropper and the tiny bits of shrimp Allen forced into him. "You're tormenting the bird."

"Mother, I've got to try."

That evening Mr. Larson came to see how Ding was

faring. He shook his head over the dusty feathers and the limp wings.

The wind rushed at the house, hurling rain at the windowpanes. Allen lay on his bed trying to read, but he was listening, waiting for a strange, dreadful sound he had never before heard. Above the noise of the storm he became conscious of a scraping and a scratching in the carton. He leapt to the box to see Ding energetically pulling himself from corner to corner. Allen ran downstairs.

"I think Ding's getting better," he called. "He's moving all around his box again."

His parents and Mr. Larson followed him up the stairs. Eleanor, who had come from her room, stood at the side of the big carton box. She was crying.

Ding lay near the green bowl filled with seawater, wings spread and limp. The bright eye was open, but his head was on the floor.

Outside in the dark the rain pelted the roof, a tree branch scratched the screen, but the breakers pounding

on the shore were too far away to be heard. They left the room quickly, silently returning to the warm fireplace downstairs. Clyde Larson asked if he could have Ding.

"I'll do an autopsy and perhaps we can see exactly why he died. Then I'll mount him for my students, and he won't be completely dead." Allen consented, mute.

"He was spunky," Mr. Charles said. "Even when he was soaked with oil and starving, those eyes looked at the world bright as buttons."

"It was the oil, of course, that killed him," Mr. Larson said. "He absorbed it through his skin, and he ate it when he preened."

"I tried hard to keep that bird alive. I did everything I could think of and more besides. But he died." Allen looked at the carpet by his feet.

"He was doomed the moment he swam into the slick," Mr. Larson said.

"Don't feel so bad, Allen," his mother reached out

and put her hand on his arm for a moment. She turned to Mr. Larson. "He's always been crazy about birds. Cars and birds are his two passions."

"Every time I buy a gallon of gas I'm encouraging somebody to drill for more oil and make more slicks," Allen said bitterly. He covered his face with his hands briefly. "I have such a headache. . . Ding was lucky. He had no questions to answer."

"Allen," Mr. Charles looked at his son. "Ding was doomed before you found him. Tell me, what would you do if you saw another oil-soaked bird on the beach tomorrow?"

"Dad, what could I do? I'd bring him home, of course." Allen paused and looked into the fire. "I guess that's always the question, 'What shall I do?' and the answer is always, 'What I can.'"

Eleanor watched the flames jump and flicker and change color.

"Ding was beautiful," she said.

ABOUT THE AUTHOR

HARRIETT MANDELAY LUGER was born in Vancouver, British Columbia. She received her B.A. degree in English literature at the University of California in Los Angeles.

"I wrote *Bird of the Farallons* because my son, Allen, brought Ding home from the beach —a mysterious emissary from a world we had peered at through the safe window of the TV screen. He belonged to the wide, wild world of the open sea and the windswept cliff. He was real. He was exotic. He was in our house. We had to find out who he was."

Mrs. Luger lives in Torrance, California, with her husband, a botanist. They have two daughters and a son.

ABOUT THE ARTIST

MICHAEL HAMPSHIRE grew up on the Yorkshire moors in England and studied art at Leeds University. Before devoting all of his time to book illustration, Mr. Hampshire taught stage design at Marymount College in Tarrytown, New York.

His great interest in wildlife and archeology has taken him to such faraway places of the world as India, Ceylon, Africa, Egypt and Central America. When he is not traveling in search of old ruins or animals, he lives in New York City.